NATIONAL GEOGRAPHIC

Energy at the Airport

ENERGY

Greg Banks

PICTURE CREDITS
Cover: 747 landing on runway, Corbis.

page 1 © So Hing-Keung/Corbis/Tranz; page 4 (bottom left)
© Michael Pohuski/FoodPix/Getty Images; page 4 (bottom right),
Digital Vision; page 5 (top) © Lawrence Manning/Corbis/Tranz;
page 5 (bottom left), PhotoAlto; page 5 (bottom right), Photodisc;
page 6 © VCL/Taxi/Getty Images; page 7 (top left) © George Hall/
Corbis/Tranz; page 7 (top center), Digital Vision; page 7 (top right)
© John H. Clark/Corbis/Tranz; page 7 (bottom left) © Yang Liu/
Corbis/Tranz; page 7 (bottom right) © Ralf-Finn Hestoft/Corbis/
Tranz; pages 8–9, Corbis; page 10, Digital Vision; page 11
© courtesy of Human Factors Group, School of Engineering,
Cranfield University, Bedford; page 14 (top) © Cameron/Corbis/
Tranz; page 14 (bottom) © Russell Munson/Corbis/Tranz; page 15
(top) © Chris Sorensen/Corbis/Tranz; page 15 (bottom) © Austin
Brown/Stone/Getty Images; page 16 © Brownie Harris/Corbis/
Tranz; page 19 (top left), Photodisc; page 19 (top right) © Frank
Cezus/Taxi/Getty Images; page 19 (bottom left) © Chris
Sorensen/Corbis/Tranz; page 19 (bottom right) © Firefly
Productions/Corbis/Tranz; page 21 © Bettmann/Corbis/Tranz;
page 22, Corbis; page 23 © Roger Ressmeyer/Corbis/Tranz;
page 24 © Sergei Guneyev/Getty Images; page 25 © Roger
Ressmeyer/Corbis/Tranz; page 26 © Joseph Sohm; ChromoSohm
Inc./Corbis/Tranz; page 29 © Charles Gupton/Corbis/Tranz.

Produced through the worldwide resources of the National
Geographic Society, John M. Fahey, Jr., President and Chief
Executive Officer; Gilbert M. Grosvenor, Chairman of the Board;
Nina D. Hoffman, Executive Vice President and President, Books
and Education Publishing Group.

PREPARED BY NATIONAL GEOGRAPHIC SCHOOL PUBLISHING
Ericka Markman, Senior Vice President and President, Children's
Books and Education Publishing Group; Steve Mico, Vice President
and Editorial Director; Marianne Hiland, Executive Editor; Richard
Easby, Editorial Manager; Jim Hiscott, Design Manager; Kristin
Hanneman, Illustrations Manager; Matt Wascavage, Manager of
Publishing Services; Sean Philpotts, Production Manager.

EDITORIAL MANAGEMENT
Morrison BookWorks, LLC

PROGRAM CONSULTANTS
Dr. Shirley V. Dickson, Program Director, Literacy, Education
Commission of the States; James A. Shymansky, E. Desmond Lee
Professor of Science Education, University of Missouri-St. Louis.

National Geographic Theme Sets program developed by Macmillan
Education Australia, Pty Limited.

Published by the National Geographic Society
1145 17th Street, N.W.
Washington, D.C. 20036-4688

ISBN: 0-7922-4776-0

Product 42016

Printed in Hong Kong.

2008 2007 2006 2005
1 2 3 4 5 6 7 8 9 10 11 12 13 14 15

Contents

Energy

Think of all the things that move. People move their bodies. Cars drive along the road. Rain falls to the ground. But do you know what is involved in all this movement? The answer is energy. Energy is involved in everything that happens. Energy is all around you. You will find energy in your home, in factories, at airports, and in sports arenas.

Key Concepts

1. Energy is the ability to do work.
2. There are different forms and sources of energy.
3. Energy can change from one form to another.

Where Energy Is Found

Energy in the Home

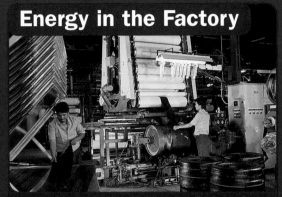

Energy can be found in the home, such as in household appliances.

Energy in the Factory

Energy in factories can be found in factory machines.

In this book you will learn about sources and users of energy at the airport, such as these airplanes.

Energy at the Airport

Energy at airports exists in computers and airplanes.

Energy at the Sports Arena

Energy is everywhere at sports arenas, such as in athletes and equipment.

Energy at the Airport

Airports are busy places. They are often crowded with people who are coming from and going to different places. Planes of all sizes take off and land. Vehicles take baggage to the planes, and signs tell people where to go. Some computers issue tickets and boarding passes. Other computers tell pilots when it is safe to land. There are many people and machines that make all this happen. But all these things need energy. Without energy, airports would not be able to function.

Things in an airport get energy from several different sources. Machines and computers get their energy from electricity. Overhead signs that display flight information also get energy from electricity. Think of all the lighting fixtures it takes to provide light to an airport. People need light to see. Pilots need lights on a runway so they can land planes safely. All these lights use energy from electricity. Trucks get energy from gasoline. Planes use huge amounts of airplane fuel in order to fly.

Runway lights help pilots land planes safely.

Here are some items you might find in and around an airport that use energy. Name several others that you may find at an airport.

Energy Users at the Airport

Airplanes

Conveyor belts

Baggage vehicles

Support vehicles

Computers

Energy, Force, and Work

Scientists define **energy** as the ability to do **work**. To understand this relationship between energy and work, you first need to understand how **force** and work are related.

> **energy**
> the ability to do work

In science, work is done when force is used to move, stop, or change something. So every time a person or a machine uses force to move, stop, or change something, work is being done. When people at an airport use force to push baggage carts or lift suitcases, they are doing work. When a conveyor belt uses force to move luggage, it is doing work. But to use force to do this work, people and machines need energy.

> **work**
> what results when force moves, stops, or changes an object

People use energy at airports when they lift their luggage.

8

If something is moved, stopped, or changed in some way, work is being done. But if nothing is moved, stopped, or changed, then no work is done. The more work that is done, the more energy is required. For example, a strong wind has more energy than a gentle breeze. The wind can put forth more force and do more work. A strong tail wind pushes in the same direction as a plane is moving. The wind's energy works with the plane's engines to make the plane fly faster. The energy of a strong head wind, on the other hand, works against the forward motion of the plane. A strong head wind will slow the plane down.

A glider is a type of airplane that has no engine. It uses the wind's energy to glide and soar.

Basic Forms of Energy

There are two basic forms of energy. One form depends on the motion of things, the other on the position of things.

Kinetic Energy The first basic form of energy is called **kinetic energy**. Kinetic energy is the energy of motion. All moving objects have kinetic energy. A person running to catch a plane has kinetic energy. You may think people standing in line waiting to buy tickets have no kinetic energy because they are not moving. But inside their bodies their hearts are beating and blood is circulating through their veins. So even a **stationary** person has kinetic energy.

The amount of kinetic energy an object has can change. The faster an object moves, the more kinetic energy it has. Kinetic energy also increases as the **mass** of an object increases. In other words, a heavy and fast-moving object has more kinetic energy than a light and slow-moving object.

These people and their baggage cart have kinetic energy as they race through the airport.

Potential Energy The other basic form of energy is called **potential energy**. Potential energy is energy that is stored. When potential energy is released, it can do work.

Think of an emergency drill on a training airplane. People acting as passengers exit the plane via inflatable slides. Each person has potential energy as she sits at the top of the slide. The amount of the passenger's potential energy depends on her position. If she is at the top of a long, high slide of a large plane, she has more potential energy than if she is at the top of a short, low slide of a smaller plane. The amount of potential energy will also change depending on the person's mass. An adult at the top of the slide has more potential energy than a child at the top of the same slide. When the person begins to move, her energy begins to change. It changes from stored potential energy to the kinetic energy of motion.

In an emergency drill, a person has potential energy at the top of the slide.

Some Sources of Energy

Energy can be stored and released in different ways.

Chemical Energy Airplane fuel is an example of a stored, or potential, chemical energy. The fuel is made up of **atoms**, and energy is stored in the **chemical bonds**, or connecting forces, between these atoms. When the fuel is ignited, or burned, the chemical bonds break apart, releasing energy. The chemical energy released from the fuel provides the energy needed to run the engines of airplanes.

Electrical Energy Think of all the equipment, lights, and computers that are used in an airport. Many of these use electrical energy to work. Electricity involves the movement of small particles called **electrons**. An electron is one of the particles that make up an atom. As the electrons move along a **circuit**, they release, or transfer, electrical energy.

Electrical energy travels to airports along power lines. These power lines are part of a giant circuit. This giant circuit connects places that make electricity, called power stations, to all the places that need electrical energy.

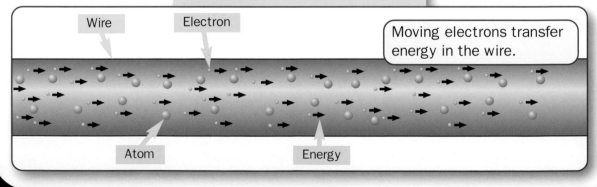

Movement of Electrical Energy

Wire

Electron

Moving electrons transfer energy in the wire.

Atom

Energy

Heat Energy It is nice to relax with a hot drink while you are waiting for a plane. The drink is hot because it has energy added to it. All things are made up of clusters of atoms called **molecules**. If heat is added, the molecules begin to move faster. We use temperature to measure how fast the molecules are moving. High temperatures mean the molecules are moving fast and have more energy. Hot drinks have a higher temperature than cold drinks, so the molecules in a hot drink are moving faster.

Heat Flow in Matter

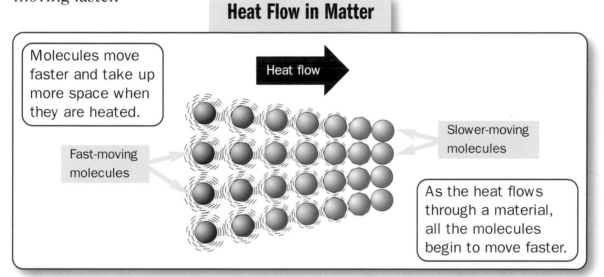

Molecules move faster and take up more space when they are heated.

Heat flow

Fast-moving molecules

Slower-moving molecules

As the heat flows through a material, all the molecules begin to move faster.

Light Energy There is one form of energy you can see. It is called light energy. Light energy travels in waves from a light source. It travels at the very fast speed of about 300,000 kilometers (186,416 miles) per second. That is fast enough to circle Earth seven times in one second.

The sun is the source of most light. But airports rely on thousands of light fixtures to provide light inside buildings and on the runways. Airports also use **lasers** to scan information from tickets. Lasers are concentrated beams of light that can be used for many tasks.

How Energy Changes

Energy does not always stay in one form. It can change from one form to another. For example, energy changes when the lights are switched on in an airport. Electrical energy moves through wires to the light bulb. Some of the electrical energy is given up to a wire in the light bulb called a **filament**. The filament gets hot enough to glow and give off light. So the electrical energy has changed first to heat energy and then to light energy.

Electrical energy changes form in a light bulb.

Runway lights guide airplane pilots in the dark.

When energy changes from one form to another, different things can happen. When a pilot starts the engines of a plane, some of the chemical energy in the fuel turns to kinetic energy as the plane begins to move. But some of the chemical energy stored in the fuel also changes to other sources of energy, such as sound and heat energy. The sound energy is the noise you hear from the engines. The blast of hot air from the engines is heat energy.

Airplane fuel has chemical energy.

Chemical energy stored in an airplane's fuel changes to kinetic energy as the plane moves. But some of it also changes to heat energy and sound energy.

Energy Change and Loss of Efficiency

When energy changes from one form to another, the process is never 100 percent **efficient**. In other words, not all the energy that is changed remains useful. The result is that when energy changes form, there is less energy to do work.

Not all the chemical energy in an airplane's fuel is changed to kinetic energy when the plane moves. Some of the chemical energy becomes sound energy and heat energy. This energy is not useful.

Scientists and engineers are constantly trying to make energy use more efficient. They are working to design new engines that would convert more of the chemical energy in fuel to kinetic energy. The result would be that planes would travel further on the same amount of fuel. The more kinetic energy an engine has, the more efficient it will be.

A engineer working on an airplane engine

Think About the Key Concepts

Think about what you read. Think about the pictures and diagrams. Use these to answer the questions. Share what you think with others.

1. What is force? How is force related to energy and work?

2. Tell how the two basic forms of energy are different from each other.

3. Name two sources of energy and give an example of how each one works.

4. What are some examples of energy changing form?

Photograph Montage

A photograph montage is a collection of photographs. The photographs show different things related to the same topic. The caption tells you what each photograph shows.

The photograph montage on page 19 shows different sources of energy that are found or used in the airport. Look back at the photograph montage on page 7. It shows different objects found in the airport that use energy.

How to Read a Photograph Montage

1. Read the title.

The title tells you the topic of the photograph montage.

2. Read the caption.

The caption tells you what each photograph shows.

3. Think about what you have learned.

Think about how the different photographs are related to each other. Think of any other photographs that could fit well into the photograph montage.

Sources of Energy at the Airport

1. Hot drink – heat energy; 2. Departure board – light energy; 3. Airplane fuel – chemical energy; 4. Runway lights – light energy

Study the Montage

Study the photograph montage by following the steps on page 18. Write down the different sources of energy that are found at the airport. Write down another example of each source of energy in the airport. Share your ideas with a classmate.

Pro-Con Articles

A pro-con article gives information on both sides of a problem or issue. The "pro" side has arguments in favor of the issue. The "con" side has arguments against the issue. The article does not try to persuade readers about the issue. Readers must make up their own minds after reading through all the arguments.

A pro-con article usually contains the following elements:

Introduction
The introduction explains the issue and gives background information to help readers understand it. The introduction may be three or four paragraphs long.

Body Paragraphs
The first few body paragraphs present the "pro" arguments. The next few body paragraphs present the "con" arguments.

The Conclusion
The conclusion briefly summarizes both sides of the issue.

Nuclear Energy

Nuclear power is used to produce electricity in many parts of the world, including the United States. The places that produce the electricity are called nuclear power stations. Nuclear power stations use a metal called uranium as fuel. Uranium forms in rocks over millions of years.

Making Electricity from Nuclear Energy

Nuclear energy is produced by splitting uranium atoms. All materials are made up of atoms. Uranium atoms are split in a power station called a reactor. When the atoms are split, a large amount of heat energy is released. This heat energy is then used to heat water to make steam. The steam is used to turn giant wheels called turbines. The turning motion of the turbines generates electricity. Nuclear power produces about 20 percent of the electricity in the United States.

The **introduction** explains the issue and gives background information.

Nuclear power plants use uranium to produce electricity.

Subheads break the information into easy-to-find sections.

Photographs tell the story of the topic in pictures.

Many people think that nuclear energy is an efficient, cost-effective way to produce electricity. However, many other people believe that the process of creating electricity from nuclear energy is too dangerous. These people believe that the risks involved are not worth taking.

The following material outlines the arguments for and against the use of nuclear energy.

Advantages of Using Nuclear Energy

Here are some of the advantages of using nuclear energy to produce electricity.

Nuclear energy is inexpensive to produce.

It takes only a very small amount of uranium to produce large amounts of electricity. Compare this to using coal to heat water into steam, a similar method of creating electricity. Much more coal than uranium is needed to create the same amount of power. As a result, the costs of using coal are much greater.

> The first few **body paragraphs** present the "pro" side, or arguments in favor of the issue.

Nuclear energy is an efficient method of producing electricity.

Once uranium is mined, it does not form again quickly in the Earth. For this reason, it is called a nonrenewable resource. However, a machine called a breeder reactor makes it possible to reuse uranium many times. Using this machine could mean that Earth's uranium will last for thousands of years.

Nuclear power plants do not pollute.

Nuclear power plants produce electricity without disturbing the environment. Unlike coal-driven plants, they do not give off harmful gases that pollute the air. Unlike windmills that produce electricity with wind power, nuclear power plants run quietly. They do not cause noise pollution.

Nuclear power makes up 20 percent of the electricity produced in the United States.

Nuclear power plants can be built almost anywhere.

Nuclear power plants usually require water to cool off their parts. However, they can actually be built almost anywhere. Nuclear power plants take up a fairly small amount of land. They have no special weather requirements.

In contrast, hydroelectric power plants, which run on water, need to be near rivers. They also need regular rainfall to keep the rivers flowing. To produce large amounts of wind-generated electricity, many windmills must be built on huge areas of land.

The Millstone Nuclear Power Station on Long Island Sound, Connecticut.

Here are some of the disadvantages of using nuclear energy to produce electricity.

Uranium is radioactive.

This is the main and most serious reason for not using nuclear energy to produce electricity.

Radioactive means that atoms, or very small particles that make up the uranium, give off an energy called radiation. Radiation is useful for heating water to create electricity. However, radiation can also be very dangerous. Radiation can affect the cells in people's bodies. This may lead to cancer. If blood cells are affected by radiation, the cells may be unable to fight off infections. In the worst cases this can lead to death. Radiation can also cause birth defects by changing the cells of unborn babies.

Nuclear accidents do happen.

Nuclear power plant workers take great care to ensure that people are not exposed to radiation. However, accidents have happened and may happen again. The worst accident was a fire and explosion in a nuclear plant in Chernobyl, Russia, in 1986. Large amounts of radiation were released into the environment. Thousands of people, animals, and plants for many miles around were killed. Many other people became seriously ill from the radiation. Many children born near Chernobyl after the accident had severe birth defects. Scientists believe that people will continue to be affected by radiation at Chernobyl for many years.

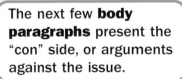

The next few **body paragraphs** present the "con" side, or arguments against the issue.

Children born near Chernobyl can be affected by radiation.

Nuclear waste materials may leak from containers.

The radioactive waste from nuclear power plants is stored in lead containers under the ground. Many people fear that these containers could leak into the environment. These leaks could occur now or in the future. Leakages would affect water, plants, and animals in the area. If people drank the water and ate the plants, the radioactive waste would affect them as well.

Uranium mining leaves behind dangerous dust.

When uranium is taken from rock in the ground, a very fine dust is left behind. This dust is made up of rock and uranium. It is also radioactive. Since the radioactive dust is left on Earth's surface, it can be blown by the wind. It can also be washed by the rain into water supplies. This poses a risk to the environment and to people.

Steel drums containing radioactive waste at Hanford Nuclear Reservation, eastern Washington

In Conclusion

There are strong arguments for and against the use of nuclear energy in electricity production. Nuclear energy is inexpensive. It uses uranium efficiently, and it does not cause air pollution. For these reasons, people who support nuclear energy believe that we should continue to use it to create electricity.

Other people believe that sooner or later, another accident like Chernobyl will happen. Then thousands more lives would be lost. In addition, waste from nuclear power plants and uranium mining sites cannot be controlled. This waste could seriously affect people and the environment in the future. People against nuclear power believe that the risks involved with nuclear power are too great. They believe we should be using other methods of electricity production.

The governments of the world need to think carefully about using nuclear power to generate electricity. They must weigh the advantages of using nuclear power against the disadvantages. Choices made now will have an important effect on the future of the world.

> The **conclusion** briefly summarizes both sides of the issue.

Steam rises from a nuclear cooling tower.

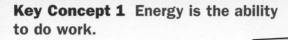

Apply the **Key Concepts**

Key Concept 1 Energy is the ability to do work.

Activity

Think of two machines that use energy to do work in an airport. Draw pictures of these machines and label them. Then write a short sentence explaining the type of work each machine does.

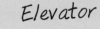

Elevator

Key Concept 2 There are different forms and sources of energy.

Activity

Make a chart about energy in the airport. In the first column, list four ways that energy can be stored and released. In the second column, list an example in the airport of each of these sources of energy. Label your chart "Types of Energy at the Airport."

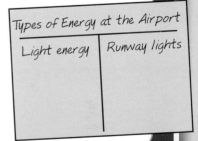

Types of Energy at the Airport	
Light energy	Runway lights

Key Concept 3 Energy can change from one form to another.

Activity

Think of a process that happens in the airport that involves an energy change. Write a sentence to describe each stage. Note the type of energy that is present at each stage.

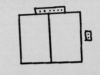

Airplane

Fuel stored in a fuel tank is chemical energy. The chemical energy changes to sound and kinetic energy when the airplane engine is turned on.

Write Your Own Pro-Con Article

You have read about the pros and cons of using nuclear energy to make electricity. Now, you can research another use of natural resources to get energy. Get ready to write your own pro-con article.

1. Study the Model

Look back at pages 21–26. Study the organization of the article. Notice how the introduction explains how nuclear energy is used to make electricity. Now look at the first several body paragraphs. They present reasons for using nuclear energy. The next several body paragraphs give reasons not to use nuclear energy. The paper ends with a conclusion that summarizes both points of view. You will want to follow this organization in your own pro-con article.

2. Choose Your Topic

Think about all the different resources people can use to make electricity. They may use water energy, coal energy, or solar energy. Choose one of these ways to make electricity that you are interested in. Your article will be about the pros and cons of using this resource to make electricity.

Writing a Pro-Con Article

◆ Write two or three introductory paragraphs that give background information.

◆ Write several "pro" paragraphs that give arguments in favor of the issue.

◆ Next, write several "con" paragraphs that give arguments against the issue.

◆ Summarize both sides of the issue in your conclusion.

3. Research Your Topic

Start by getting background information about your resource. Use the library or the Internet. Find out how long the resource has been used and how many people get electricity from it. Next, look for pro and con information about the resource. Find three or four things that make it a good source of electricity. Then find three or four reasons not to use it. Look for information about cost, how much of the resource is available, and issues with the environment. Organize your points in a chart.

Using Water Energy

Pros	Cons
• reusable resource	• damages the environment

4. Write a Draft

Look over the information you have found. Put the important background facts into your introduction. Then write the pro and con arguments. Present the same number of pro points as con points. Finally, write a conclusion that summarizes both sides of the argument.

5. Revise and Edit

Read your draft. Does it give good background information? Make sure it shows each side of the issue fairly. Correct any mistakes in your spelling or punctuation.

Hold an Energy Debate

A debate is a meeting where two people or groups each present and defend a different side of an argument. Now that you have written about a type of energy, you can get together with other students who wrote on the same topic and have an energy debate.

How to Hold a Debate

1. Form topic groups.

Form groups according to the writing topic. Then divide these groups into two: those students who will discuss the pro side and those who will discuss the con side.

2. Organize your information.

Work in these small groups to develop a pro or con argument on your energy topic. Make a list of all the pros or cons each member of the group thought of.

3. Plan your argument.

As a group, decide which pros or cons would make the strongest argument. Organize these issues into a presentation.

4. Get ready to present your pro or con argument.

Choose a person from the group to be the speaker. This person can practice reading the argument while other group members give feedback. Those who are not presenting should prepare to answer questions from the class.

5. Present your pro or con arguments.

The two speakers from either side of the issue will present their arguments to the class. The rest of the class can ask questions of the other group members once both sides of the argument have been presented. Then the class can vote on which side gave the strongest argument on the issue.

Glossary

atoms – the tiniest units of matter

chemical bonds – forces that hold atoms together to form molecules

circuit – the path along which an electric current moves

efficient – being effective with little energy or time wasted

electrons – the smallest parts that make up an atom

energy – the ability to do work

filament – the thin wire inside a light bulb that gives off light energy when heated

force – something that causes, changes, or stops the movement of an object

kinetic energy – the energy of motion

lasers – objects that make very narrow beams of strong light

mass – the amount of matter in an object

molecules – small parts of matter, made up of two or more atoms

potential energy – stored energy

stationary – not moving

work – what results when force moves, stops, or changes an object

Index